My Name is Olivia

A Collection of Stories
about People who Share my Name

By Allison Dearstyne

For every girl named Olivia. May you always be a peacemaker!

The name Olivia comes from the Latin word "oliva," which means "olive" or "olive tree." In ancient Rome, olive trees symbolized peace and friendship. To this day, the phrase "extend an olive branch" means reach out in reconciliation. It's possible the name Olivia first meant friendship and peace. Olivia also is a feminine form of the boy's name Oliver. William Shakespeare made your name popular when he created a character named Olivia in his play "Twelfth Night."

Did you know that there have been extraordinary women who share your name through history? We will look at these seven outstanding heroes named Olivia:

Olivia Poole

Olivia Davidson Washington

Olivia Choong

Olivia Hooker

Olivia Breen

Olivia Ward Bush-Banks

Olivia Bouler

Olivia Poole was the American Indian inventor of a baby swing. She was born in North Dakota in 1889 to parents who were part Ojibway. Olivia grew up on the White Earth Indian Reserve in Minnesota learning tribal customs that one day inspired her clever invention.

For thousands of years, Ojibway mothers strapped their babies to cradle boards called papooses. Tiny babies feel comforted when they are swaddled up tight. When the mothers worked outdoors, they tied the papooses to sturdy tree branches using leather straps. Then they lightly tugged the branches, so the papooses bounced gently. It soothed the babies while the mothers worked.

When Olivia grew up, she went to college in Canada, married a man named Delbert and had a baby named Joseph. Remembering the bouncing papooses, Olivia created something similar for Joseph from objects around her house. Olivia used a broom handle instead of a branch, and a cloth diaper instead of a papoose. She had a blacksmith create a steel spring that allowed Joseph to swing low enough for his toes to touch the ground and push himself upward. That way, he could create the bouncing motion all by himself and make his muscles strong at the same time. Baby Joseph loved his swing! Olivia and Delbert had six more children and they used her bouncy swing for each of them, making improvements on it over time.

Later, Olivia made bouncy swings for her grandchildren. In 1948, Olivia's family convinced her that her invention was genius, and she should patent and sell it everywhere! A patent is something you get for an invention that legally protects you from other people copying your idea and selling it. Olivia patented her invention and started a company to mass produce her bouncy swing with Joseph's help. She named her swing the "Jolly Jumper" and became one of the first Canadian Indigenous women to patent an invention.

The Jolly Jumper became wildly popular, and parents everywhere called it a lifesaver! You probably bounced in some version of a Jolly Jumper long before you can remember. Inventors look for ways to make life easier and solve problems with creative thinking. Think about things you can invent to make life easier, and you can be like clever Olivia Poole!

Olivia Davidson Washington was the cofounder of Tuskegee Institute, along with her husband, Booker T. Washington. She was born in Virginia in 1854, the daughter of an ex-slave. When Olivia was little, life was dangerous for free Black Virginians, so her family moved north, eventually to Albany, New York.

Albany was known for its anti-slavery movement and young Olivia met a lot of people, both Black and White, who worked hard to end slavery. She attended a school that was owned and operated by Black Americans. Olivia's upbringing led her to become both a teacher and a changemaker. While she lived in the North, the American Civil War began and ended in a Union victory, making slavery illegal.

Olivia got her first teaching job in Ohio when she was 16. Two years later, she moved to Mississippi to teach freed adults and their children. She had a heart for improving the lives of girls through education. Back then, most people didn't see value in educating girls like Olivia did. Lucy Webb Hayes, the wife of President Rutherford Hayes, saw the tremendous impact Olivia had on her students and gave her a college scholarship.

At Olivia's college graduation, she delivered a speech and met Booker T. Washington, another speaker there. He was a changemaker like Olivia! The two formed a working relationship and decided to create a school for higher education for Black Americans. They founded Tuskegee Institute in Alabama, which gave young adults skills to work in different types of jobs.

Olivia fund-raised, taught and became a principal who oversaw female students on campus. She was an equal partner to Booker, who gave Olivia credit for Tuskegee Institute's great success. After they founded the school, they both experienced personal struggles. Booker's wife died and Olivia became very sick. Still, she worked at the school through her illness. Booker asked Olivia to marry him, and she said yes! She was a loving stepmother to his daughter, and later she had two sons.

Olivia and Booker accomplished so much together. Olivia saw great value in educating girls, so when you are in school, pay close attention and you can be like amazing Olivia Davidson Washington!

Olivia Choong is an environmental activist from Singapore. She was born in 1979. Olivia studied mass communication and public relations in college and learned skills that helped her protect our planet! Pollution and waste have made the earth sick. We all need to work together to make the earth healthier. One way to do that is to live sustainably.

Sustainable living means working to reduce the use of Earth's natural resources as a lifestyle. You've probably heard phrases like "going green" and "reduce, reuse, recycle." These are mottos for living sustainably. People who live sustainably change their home designs, transportation, energy use and diet to live better with the earth. They live simply and become self-reliant, especially with the food they eat. Olivia teaches people how to do that on a small scale and works with companies to do that on a large scale.

Usually, businesses that help the environment are small and have a hard time growing. It's expensive for businesses to go green. So, Olivia created two companies to help businesses help the planet. The companies are called Green Drinks and Green PR. They give expert advice to businesses on environmental issues. Olivia's companies work with the government and the public to help the earth. Her companies make it a lot easier for businesses to use sustainable practices.

Olivia is also into urban farming. People don't typically think of cities as good spaces for gardening, but Olivia proves that gardens can thrive even in unusual spaces! She has a website called "The Tender Gardener," which shows how she lives sustainably by farming and caring for chickens. In 2013, Olivia was recognized on a national level when she received the EcoFriend award for her work.

These days, there are many social media platforms and people can go viral for all kinds of things. Olivia is using her platform to help the earth. She says that her personal mission is to form connections between people and creation care. Think about ways that you can live more sustainably, and you can help the earth too, just like Olivia Choong!

Olivia Hooker was the first Black woman to serve in active duty in the United States Coast Guard. She was born in 1915 in Oklahoma. Back then, segregation was legal. You've probably seen pictures of segregation. Black people could not drink from the same water fountains as White people. The best seats were always reserved for White people even if Black people got there first. It wasn't fair!

In Tulsa, where Olivia lived, many Black people owned successful businesses despite segregation. She was six years old when racist ways of life turned extremely violent. Angry over a made-up rumor, White mobs stormed through her neighborhood and wrecked things owned by Black people. They destroyed furniture in Olivia's home and burned down her father's clothing store.

Olivia remembered, "I guess the most shocking thing was seeing people, to whom you had never done anything to irritate, who just took it upon themselves to destroy your property because they didn't want you to have those things. And they were teaching you a lesson. Those were all new ideas to me."

Immediately after the terrible events in Tulsa, White city officials hid evidence, and no one was charged with a crime. The victims and their families never received money from insurance companies or the government for all that they had lost. Like many other Black Tulsans, Olivia's family moved afterwards. Her parents always urged her to not agonize over the past, but to look forward and try to make things better.

When Olivia grew up, she went to college and became an elementary school teacher. Then life changed for Americans in 1941 when Japan attacked Pearl Harbor, drawing the United States into World War II. There was a shortage of men to work in their usual jobs because so many of them were fighting overseas. So, women filled their positions in the workforce. For the first time, the United States military opened its ranks to women, and Olivia enlisted. In 1945, Olivia became the first Black woman accepted into the Coast Guard.

After the war, Olivia earned her master's degree and doctorate degree in psychology. She worked with children with physical and intellectual disabilities, and she cofounded an organization that advocated for them. Advocates help people by speaking on their behalf. Olivia was also a professor at Fordham University for 23 years.

Throughout her life, Olivia publicly spoke about her early memories in Tulsa. As an old lady, she testified before Congress, asking for proper acknowledgement and money to be granted to those who had lost so much. Olivia never stopped advocating for people who needed her help!

President Barack Obama honored 100-year-old Olivia when he spoke at the Coast Guard Academy, calling her "a tireless voice for justice and equality." Olivia Hooker was unstoppable! She was a trailblazer and an advocate. At some point, you likely will be able to advocate for someone who needs your help. Take the opportunity and you can be like courageous Olivia Hooker!

Olivia "Livvy" Breen is a Welsh Paralympian. She was born a twin in 1996 in England. In the hospital, baby Livvy became very sick and had to stay in the hospital for a month. When she went home, she didn't thrive like her twin brother. Livvy was late to crawl and walk, and she was diagnosed with Cerebral Palsy when she was two.

Cerebral Palsy is a disorder that deals with movement. People who have Cerebral Palsy can have a variety of symptoms, but the most common symptoms are poor coordination, weak, stiff muscles and tremors. Livvy is also hard of hearing and has learning disabilities. When she was little, she never wanted to view herself as disabled or different from other kids

Livvy always struggled in school but became a fast runner. Her favorite day in school was Sports Day because she got to shine! When she was 13, she joined a local athletic club and got to compete in national championships for disabled athletes. During these competitions, Livvy began to accept her Cerebral Palsy as a positive part of who she was.

Livvy was so fast she made it to the Paralympic Games, becoming the second youngest athlete on her team in the United Kingdom to compete. The Paralympic Games are an international multi-sport event. It's like the Olympics except every athlete has a disability.

Livvy was given an athletic scholarship to train for her events. It took years of hard work, and she competed in two Paralympic Games. Livvy set world records in the long jump - 5.15 meters! She also medaled in running events, sprinting 100 meters in 12.76 seconds. In 2018, Livvy was named the Disability Sport Wales Female Athlete of the Year.

Every serious athlete is strong and disciplined. It takes even more strength and discipline to be a disabled athlete like Livvy. Olivia Breen helps us remember to never underestimate people with disabilities!

Olivia Ward Bush Banks was a Montauk and Black American poet, playwright, historian and founder of a school. The Montauk tribe is a Native American tribe indigenous to Long Island. Olivia was born in 1869 in Long Island, New York.

When she was in high school, a drama teacher recognized Olivia's talent. She gave Olivia private lessons that proved one day to be very useful to her. Olivia married shortly after high school and had two daughters, but her marriage was unhappy and ended in divorce.

To support her daughters, Olivia worked a variety of jobs, mostly relating to editing or drama in some way. One way she earned income was writing and publishing poetry. Olivia is best known for a volume of poetry called *Driftwood*. This poem called "Voices" is from *Driftwood*:

I stand upon the haunted plain
Of vanished day and year,
And ever o'er its gloomy waste
Some strange, sad voice I hear.
Some voice from out the shadowed Past;
And one I call Regret,
And one I know is Misspent Hours,
Whose memory lingers yet.

Then Failure speaks in bitter tones,
And Grief, with all its woes;
Remorse, whose deep and cruel stings
My painful thoughts disclose.
Thus do these voices speak to me,
And flit like shadows past;
My spirit falters in despair,
And tears flow thick and fast.

But when, within the wide domain
Of Future Day and Year
I stand, and o'er its sunlit Plain
A sweeter word I hear,
Which bids me leave the darkened Past
And crush its memory,--
I'll hasten to obey the Voice
Of Opportunity.

Many of Olivia's poems celebrate American heroes and focus on the achievements of Black Americans. There was an event that likely moved her to write about her Montauk heritage too. In a 1910 court case, the Montauk tribe was declared extinct by the United States government, even though dozens of Montauk tribe members were in the courtroom when the verdict was announced.

After this decision, which wronged the Montauk people, Olivia wrote a play called *Indian Trails: or Trail of the Montauk* about her people. The play showcased her culture and included dialogue in the Montauk language. Olivia acted in the play too. Unfortunately, most parts of the play have been lost.

Thankfully though, Olivia's works remain as a Montauk tribal historian. Historians have an important job because they study and write about the past. Olivia used resources from her tribe's past to write about their history.

Olivia remarried and moved to Chicago. There, Olivia founded the Bush-Banks School of Expression dedicated to developing artistic and theatrical talent of young Black students. Teachers don't typically become famous or wealthy, but they can make a huge impact. Olivia inspired her students to be exceptional.

Olivia changed lives through her teaching and writing. Write about your family history and things you have experienced, and you can be like talented Olivia Ward Bush-Banks!

Olivia Bouler is a young American hero who combined her passion for art and birds to accomplish something wonderful. She grew up in New York and often vacationed on the Gulf Coast in Louisiana and Alabama with her cousins and grandparents. She always loved it there, especially the many species of birds. Olivia was an artist who spent a lot of her free time drawing and painting.

In April 2010, there was an oil spill in the Gulf of Mexico. A gas company called BP, short for British Petroleum, had an oil well that spilled 49.5 million barrels of oil into the gulf. Over 650 miles of gulf coastline were polluted, causing serious damage to all the wildlife in the area.

Olivia was only in fifth grade, but she wanted to help! She came up with an idea and reached out to the National Audubon Society, a nonprofit organization dedicated to helping the earth. Olivia pledged to create 500 pictures of birds and send them to people who contributed to disaster relief for the wildlife.

She thought, "Who knows, maybe I'll raise $200." She underestimated herself! Her story made it to big news outlets and inspired many people to donate. Around $200,000 was raised for Audubon's Gulf Coast relief and 500 donors received their original artwork by Olivia! She copied and published her paintings in her children's book *Olivia's Birds: Saving the Gulf.*

Olivia has been recognized on a national level for her efforts in the oil spill recovery. She was named a White House Champion of Change! Through middle and high school, Olivia spoke publicly to her peers about how they can be changemakers too.

We learn from Olivia Bouler that all of us can contribute to worthwhile causes. You are not too young to make a big impact!

This page is all about you!

_____ was born on

_____

As a baby, Olivia _____

_____

As a little girl, Olivia _____

_____

Olivia is especially good at _____

_____

Olivia is often described as _____

_____

Olivia makes people laugh when she _____

_____

One day Olivia would like to _____

_____

This page is for making a self-portrait. A self-portrait is a picture of you, drawn by you!

Bibliography

"About Olivia." Olivia Breen Official Website. *oliviabreen.co.uk.* Web. 08 May 2024.

Bailey, Betty. "Olivia Bouler." My Hero. *myhero.com.* 14 Apr. 2020. Web. 17 May 2024.

"Bush-Banks, Olivia Ward." Encyclopedia of World Biography. *Encycopedia.com.* 15 Apr. 2024. Web. 14 May 2024.

Choong, Olivia. "About Me." *Oliviachoong.com.* Web.13 May 2024.

Hofstaedter, Maggie. "Olivia Bouler – her passion is "For the Birds!" Inspiremykids. *inspiremykids.com.* Web. 17 May 2024.

Lawson Bush, Nana. "Olivia A. Davidson (1854-1889). Blackpast. *Blackpast.org.* 19 Jan. 2007. Web. 10 May 2024.

"Olivia." Babynames.com. *babynames.com* Web. 06 May 2024.

"Olivia Bouler's Visit." Audubon Seabird Institute. *seabirdinstitue.audubon.org.* Web. 17 May 2024.

"Olivia Hooker, 103, Dies; Witness to an Ugly Moment in History." The New York Times. *nytimes.com.* 23 Nov. 2018. Web. 16 May 2024.

"Olivia Poole." Lemelson-MIT. *lemelson.mit.edu.* Web. 07 May 2024.

Singh, Amardeep. "African American Poetry (1870-1928): A Digital Anthology." *Scalar.lehigh.edu.* Web. 13 May 2024.

Wagner, Ella. "Olivia Hooker." National Park Service. *nps.gov.* 16 Oct. 2023. Web. 16 May 2024.

Washington, Olivia Davidson (1854-1889). Women in World History: A Biographical Encyclopedia. *Encycopedia.com.* 15 Apr. 2024. Web. 10 May 2024.

Ward Bush-Banks, Olivia. "Driftwood." (Full Text) 1914. Web. 13 May 2024.

White House Author. The White House: President Barack Obama. *Obamawhitehouse.archives.gov.* Web. 17 May 2024.

Wikipedia contributors. "Olivia Choong." *Wikipedia, The Free Encyclopedia.* Wikipedia, The Free Encyclopedia, 31 Oct. 2023. Web. 13 May. 2024.

Wikipedia contributors. "Olivia Ward Bush-Banks." *Wikipedia, The Free Encyclopedia.* Wikipedia, The Free Encyclopedia, 23 Apr. 2024. Web. 13 May. 2024.

Young, Jessica. "Olivia Poole." The Canadian Encyclopedia. *Thecanadianencyclopedia.org.* 24 July 2020. Web. 07 May 2024.